COCKTAIL POPS

and Spiked Frozen Treats

Jeanne Benedict

Published by Ice Enterprises, Inc.

For more information on Jeanne Benedict
products visit www.JeanneBenedict.com

ISBN: 978-0-9910125-0-3

THANK YOU

**John,
Dylan,
and Piper**

For being
the sweetest
family ever!

CHEERS!

It's a bit naughty, the notion of our favorite frozen playground treat all grown up with a splash of sprit. From potable ice pops to spiked snow cones in a Martini glass, these Cocktail Pops have been a big hit on national TV shows, my blog, and at parties! I am thrilled to bring my recipes for frosty holiday treats and frozen nips on a stick to you in this book.

Showcasing my pops on TV has let me know exactly what kind of Cocktail Pops you want thanks to what was searched on my website after each appearance. The White Russian Ice Cream Sandwich Sliders were very popular when I introduced them on the Today Show, and the striped fruity push pops that I shared on Access Hollywood Live were big winners too.

People love to see their go-to cocktail revamped as an ice pop, and I hope you find your favorites in my book. Let me know at JeanneBenedict.com while you chill out and have a Cocktail Pop!

(Photo: Kiwi, Watermelon, Mango Daiquiri Push Pop, recipe variation on page 27)

TABLE OF CONTENTS

Dinner Party Indulgences

Holiday Cheer

Chilly Creativity

Tips from Pops Sticks to Molds to Pop-ular FAQs

Dreaming up Cocktail Pop designs has become one of my favorite pastimes. I especially enjoy pairing creative pop sticks with the perfect mold resulting in the quintessential Cocktail Pop. Can you imagine a Martini sans its iconic glass? That's how I feel about the mold-to-stick match-up! Here are some of my favorite pop stick choices, molds, and makers along with tried and true tips from freezing alcohol to keeping pops chilly on a party table.

Pop Molds & Makers

Plastic Pop Molds - Every time I see a plastic pop mold, I have to have it! Garage sales can be goldmines for retro pop forms, and I recently picked up some sleek tapered 1oz. molds at the 99-cent store. But, the place to go year-round for pop molds is Bed, Bath, and Beyond. And, the Tovolo brand always seems to have unique designs – definitely a fave!

Quick Pop Maker – Zoku Quick Pop Maker is awesome! I've been using their 3-pop mold maker for years on TV and at home. It's my first choice when making Cocktail Pops as most mixtures freeze in about 10 minutes. Plus, the mold cavities are metal so you can easily apply an edible decoration, such as mini cut-out apple stars, to the inside of the mold and create gorgeous pops. They have wonderful accessories too, like novelty mini cutters for fruit, a siphon to make core pops, and a chocolate dipping station to coat your pops.

Snow Cone & Shaved Ice Machines – Home snow cone makers seemed to be the retail darling this past summer, many priced around $20! I have the Hawaiian Shaved Ice brand of snow cone and shaved ice machine. They are easy to use and very affordable, plus this brand has lots of tasty snow cone syrups, which can be used for Cocktail Pops too.

Silicone or Flexible Molds – If you are making ice pop shot glasses or something with an unconventional shape, a flexible silicone mold is the absolute way to go. You want to be able to pull the mold of the frozen product instead of pulling it out of the mold. Trust me on this! I love the brand Fred "Cool Shooter" shot glass mold. Also, check out silicone ice cube trays and baking molds where you'll find spheres, cubes, and tons of fun stuff!

DIY Molds – Disposable plastic cups are great for pops in a pinch and plastic 1-inch wide tube bags (freezer pop bags), are a cool way to contain your pops too. You can make these bags using a food sealer or buy a box of freezer pops at the 99-cent store, empty out the bags, wash in warm water and up-cycle the bags for your homemade booze pops! Also, a genius product, Make Your Own Molds sells food-grade silicone putty and a variety of substances, so you can make a flexible mold out of just about anything. I used this product to make gummy bug molds for my Halloween Creepy Cosmo Pops (page 80). Look for this product online!

Push Pop Containers – It doesn't get much more fun than a push pop. Bonus! They hold a nice amount of hooch! Push pops have become so popular that you can find them in a variety of shapes and sizes like hearts and mini molds. Check online resources for bulk deals.

Pop Sticks

Wooden Pop Sticks (classic stick, corndog stick or dowel, coffee stirrer, ice cream spoon, mini appetizer fork or pick, tongue depressor) - These sticks are ideal when you are making lots of party pops as they are economical and disposable, compared to pop mold sticks that are made from reusable plastic. Be sure to get food-friendly sticks, and not craft sticks, which can splinter.

Chopsticks – Stylish and modern, chopsticks are available in a myriad of designs making them the perfect choice for upscale cocktail party pops. But, pops tend to slide off chopsticks due to the tapered tip, which is how I prefer to insert them into the pop. To prevent this, I usually stick a white gumdrop, or a gumdrop color compatible to the pop, on the tip; it gives the pop something to grab on to. Also, make sure the chopstick doesn't have a decorative tip that might detach when you pull out the pop, like a 1-inch metal piece. Best bet for beautiful chopsticks is Pier One.

Plastic Straws, Swizzle Sticks – Swizzles and straws usually come in bright colors and fit right into the cocktail theme. Follow the tips about Chopsticks if you find that your pops slip off the sticks and use hard plastic or Acrylic, not a flimsy plastic that could break.

Rosemary Twigs, Cinnamon Sticks – For those looking to make cozy holiday pops, you can't beat a food-friendly stick with a scent. Wash these types of sticks and twigs thoroughly, and choose thicker rosemary stems and extra long cinnamon sticks.

Pop-ular FAQs

But I thought alcohol doesn't freeze, which is why I keep my vodka in the freezer?

Untrue! Yes, alcohol on its own doesn't solidify in conventional home freezers, which on average are set at -18 Celsius / 0 Fahrenheit. For the trivia geeks, like me: ethanol alcohol, what our cocktails are made with, freezes at around -114 Celsius / -173 Fahrenheit. However, alcohol mixed with juice, sugar, water, cream etc…will freeze at home if the proportions are correct. 2 teaspoons of vodka and similar spirits is about all a 2 oz. juice-based pop can take. Liqueurs or schnapps, with their higher sugar content, allow for a more potable pop. And a pop made with pureed fruit, as are most sorbets, can really pack a punch!

How do I keep my creative pop sticks that did not come with the mold upright and centered?

I have two techniques for this. Pour 1 tablespoon of pop mixture into the molds and freeze; this way the stick tips will rest on this layer and not be visible at the top of the pops when unmolded. Then, place the pop sticks in the molds, where they'll just lean on the side for now, but you want the displacement of the sticks in the mixture. Pour the rest of the mixture in the molds and freeze until pops are a firm slush. Straighten the sticks in the mold, to where they are upright and centered, and freeze. Or, fill molds almost to the top and freeze until pops are a firm slush. Then, insert the pop sticks, so they are about 1/2-inch up from the bottom of the mold, and freeze.

How do I unmold my super frozen pops?

Hot water for about 5 seconds on the outside of plastic pop molds usually does the trick, but be careful not to get water inside the mold on the pop.

How do I get that "window pane" look with fruit shapes and décor items in my pops?

I must have made the Cosmo Pops on the front of the book 20 times, because I was not happy with the way the lime looked. The problem was that the lime appeared embedded and blurry, so I developed this technique to get a "window pane" look, as exemplified by the Kiwi Pomegranate Vodka Pop in the photo on this page. Fill your molds 3/4 full with pop mixture (reserve remaining mixture), and freeze until pops are a firm slush. Insert pop sticks and freeze completely. Then, unmold pops and place in freezer to keep firm. Re-fill each mold with 1 tablespoon of reserved mixture. Coat fruit shape or décor item in sugar glue (recipe page 13) and adhere to pops. Submerge pops back in molds, so mixture in bottom comes up around fruit or item and is level with top surface; freeze completely.

The nice thing about using plastic pop molds is that you can see where the décor item is placed and even adjust it if necessary for a precise design. If you are using a quick pop mold, which is usually made of metal, moistened fruit or décor items stick to the mold beautifully, as with the apples in my Patriotic Pops (page 76), but you can't see through metal, so you are sort of "winging it" with the final design. Plus, not everyone owns a quick pop maker, hence this "window pane" technique!

How do I keep my pops frozen and looking fab displayed on a party table?

Ice, ice baby. OK, so you may see some of my Cocktail Pops photographed without ice, but that's just for recipe reference. Ice pops will start to melt immediately after you take them out of the freezer. Want proof? Look at some of the video clips of my TV segments where I have a line-up of ice pops or frozen treats and after 3 minutes, near the end of the segment, the pops that are not on ice start melting on the table, or worse, on the host of the show. The best way to serve pops is by laying them on top of ice in a large bowl, so when the ice or pops start to melt the liquid will be contained.

To display pops on a tray or ceramic platter, fold a white paper towel to fit on the tray under the ice (the ice should completely mask the paper towel). The towel will absorb melting liquid and help keep the ice from sliding off the tray. Also, it's a good idea to put the ice in the bowl and then in the freezer for about 30 minutes, as a colder vessel will keep everything chillier.

What's the best way to transport my pops to my friend's house so she can chill out?

Dry ice! Check with grocery stores or an ice vendor in your area to purchase dry ice. Dry ice is usually sold in small slabs or pellets, typically 10 lb. minimum for @$10, and that's really all you need in a cooler to keep pops frozen. Bring the cooler with you when buying the ice. Use caution when handling dry ice; it will burn you if you touch it with bare hands. Wear heavy water-proof gloves and use metal tongs or a spoon to put the ice in your cooler. When I transport pops, I buy about 4 disposable aluminum trays that fit inside my cooler. I put one tray in the bottom and place the dry ice on top of it. I place another tray on top of that with pops in individual plastic bags and some regular ice in the tray around the pops. I layer the trays in this manner and also put thick cardboard pieces wrapped in foil at the tray corners to act as protective risers so a tray doesn't collapse on the one below it, or on to the pops! Never serve or store ice pops directly on dry ice.

Basic Syrup Recipes

You'll see these recipes many times throughout the book. They are key ingredients for pop success!

Simple Syrup

1 cup granulated sugar

1 cup water

Stir sugar and water together in a small saucepan until sugar is moistened. Cook over medium-high heat until mixture boils and sugar dissolves; about 5 minutes. Cool completely and transfer to a cruet or container with a spout. Cover and refrigerate until ready to use.

Sugar Glue for Garnishes

2 cups granulated sugar

1 cup water

Stir sugar and water together in a small saucepan until sugar is moistened. Cook over medium-high heat until mixture boils and sugar dissolves; about 5 - 8 minutes. Cool completely and transfer to a cruet or a container with a spout. Cover and refrigerate until ready to use.

COOL COCKTAILS

Screwdriver Pops

As I was creating this pop, I wondered, "How many people still belly up to the bar and order a Screwdriver?" This icy version with an array of citrus garnish could cue a makeover of the classic cocktail.

Ingredients

1 cup water

3/4 cup orange juice

1/3 cup simple syrup (recipe page 13)

2 tablespoons vodka

1/8-inch thick orange, lemon, lime slices cut into small triangles

Steps Mix together water, orange juice, simple syrup, and vodka.

Fill 6 - 8 (2 oz.) plastic molds 3/4 full with mixture and freeze until slushy; reserve remaining mixture.

Insert pop sticks when mixture is a firm slush and freeze completely.

To get a "window pane" look with citrus triangles, unmold pops and place in freezer to keep firm. Re-fill each mold with 1 tablespoon of reserved mixture. Coat triangles in sugar glue (recipe page 13) and adhere to pops. Submerge pops back in molds so mixture in bottom comes up around triangles and is level with top surface; freeze completely.

Remove pops from molds and serve on ice in a large bowl.

Makes 6 - 8 (2 oz.) pops

Long Island Iced Tea Pops

Although I've never summered in the Hamptons, these sophisticated Long Island Ice Tea Pops somehow take me there as I imagine lounging poolside with celebs at fancy fetes.

Ingredients

1 cup cola

1/2 cup cold water

1/2 cup liquid sweet and sour mixer

3 teaspoons sugar (divided)

1 teaspoon vodka

1 teaspoon rum

1 teaspoon gin

1 teaspoon Tequila

1/2 teaspoon triple sec

Lemon slices cut in 1/8-inch thick half circles

Steps Pour cola into a glass, loosely cover with plastic wrap, and let stand overnight to uncarbonate. Then, stir in 2 teaspoons of sugar, cover, and set aside.

Combine water, sweet and sour mixer, 1 teaspoon sugar, and all liquor in a bowl.

Use a pop stick to press a moistened half circle lemon slice inside each mold of a frozen quick pop maker, such as Zoku (for slow pops see "window pane" design tips on page 11). Insert pop sticks. Pour in 1 oz. of the sweet and sour mixture and freeze. Fill rest of mold with cola. (Place mold back into freezer to speed up the process.) Freeze completely and unmold.

Remove pops from molds, put in plastic bags, and keep in freezer while making more pops. Serve pops on ice in a large bowl.

Makes 6 - 8 (2 oz.) pops

Cosmopolitan Pops

You might think it odd that I specify "red" for the cranberry juice in this recipe, but cranberry juice is also available in "white," and a variety of other cran-concoctions on the grocery store shelves.

Ingredients

1 cup red cranberry juice

1/4 cup water

1/3 cup simple syrup (recipe page 13)

1 tablespoon vodka

1 teaspoon triple sec

2 teaspoons fresh lime juice

Lime slices cut in 1/8-inch thick half circles

1/2 cup orange juice

Steps Mix together cranberry juice, water, simple syrup, liquor, and lime juice.

Fill 6 (2 oz.) plastic molds 3/4 full with mixture and freeze until slushy; reserve remaining mixture.

Insert pop sticks when mixture is a firm slush and freeze completely.

To get a "window pane" look with limes, unmold pops and place in freezer to keep firm. Re-fill each mold with 1 tablespoon of reserved mixture. Coat limes in sugar glue (recipe page 13) and adhere to pops. Submerge pops back in molds so mixture in bottom comes up around limes and is level with top surface; freeze completely. Finish off design by adding a 1/2-inch layer of orange juice in mold and freeze.

Remove pops from molds and serve on ice in a large bowl.

Makes 6 (2 oz.) pops

Pina Colada Pops

I brought these Pina Colada Pops to a dinner party as dessert, and the host ate 3 pops! Serve them at a luau or summer party.

Ingredients

1 cup pineapple juice (canned)

5 tablespoons Coco Lopez Cream of Coconut

1/3 cup simple syrup (recipe page 13)

1 tablespoon sweetened flaked coconut, plus 1/4 cup for garnish

2 teaspoons dark rum

12 pineapple chunks

Steps Mix together pineapple juice, cream of coconut, simple syrup, flaked coconut, and rum.

Use a pop stick to press a couple of moistened pineapple chunks inside each mold of a frozen quick pop maker, such as Zoku (for slow pops see "window pane" design tips on page 11). Insert pop sticks. Fill mold with pina colada mixture and freeze.

Remove pops from molds, put in plastic bags, and keep in freezer while making more pops. When ready to serve, brush base of pop with simple syrup and sprinkle remaining 1/4 cup flaked coconut on syrup. Serve pops on ice in a large bowl.

Makes 6 - 8 (2 oz.) pops

Watermelon Margarita Pops

Instead of watermelon at a summer party, serve these stunning watermelon pops spiked with Tequila! I wanted these to resemble a watermelon, so I just used what was in my kitchen to create the green rind: lemonade and green food coloring. Use your imagination to get the right look if you don't have all these ingredients on hand.

Ingredients

1 1/2 cups watermelon

1 1/2 tablespoons water

1 tablespoon Tequila

2 teaspoons snow cone watermelon syrup (Hawaiian Shaved Ice brand)

1/2 cup prepared lemonade

Green food coloring

Chopped dark chocolate or chocolate chips

Steps Puree watermelon, water, and watermelon syrup in a blender. Transfer to a container with a spout, such as a large measuring cup. In another container, mix together lemonade and green food coloring.

Stir some watermelon mixture into the chocolate chips. Use a pop stick to press about 5 moistened chocolate chips inside each mold of a frozen quick pop maker, such as Zoku (for slow pops see "window pane" design tips on page 11). Insert pop sticks. Fill mold with almost to the top with watermelon mixture and freeze. Then, add green lemonade to the top fill line and freeze.

Remove pops from molds, put in plastic bags, and keep in freezer while making more pops. Serve pops on ice in a large bowl.

Makes 6 – 8 (2 oz.) pops

Melon Ball Pops

Melon Ball cocktails were definitely my first choice when I was living in New York in my twenties. This recipe celebrates that time; trying to cool off on a hot night!

Ingredients

Cantaloupe

1/2 cup orange juice

1/2 cup cold water

1/3 cup simple syrup (recipe page 13)

1 tablespoon Midori melon liqueur

1 teaspoon vodka

1 drop green food coloring (optional)

Steps Cut cantaloupe into 1/8-inch thick slices, then cut out 1/2-inch diameter circles using a mini canapé or cookie cutter.

Mix together orange juice, water, simple syrup, liquor, and food coloring.

Use a pop stick to press a few moistened cantaloupe circles inside each mold of a frozen quick pop maker, such as Zoku (for slow pops see "window pane" design tips on page 11). Insert pop sticks. Fill mold with melon mixture and freeze.

Remove pops from molds, put in plastic bags, and keep in freezer while making more pops. Serve pops on ice in a large bowl.

Makes 6 (2 oz.) pops

Mango, Lychee, Kiwi Daiquiri Push Pops

These pretty pops are super convenient in their little push pop containers. For the white layer, Lychee was an ideal choice with the exotic flavors of mango and kiwi.

Ingredients

For Kiwi Layer:

1 cup chopped fresh kiwi (peeled)

1 tablespoon frozen limeade concentrate

1 teaspoon white rum

1 teaspoon corn syrup

For Lychee Layer:

1 cup lychee (canned in syrup)

1 tablespoon frozen limeade concentrate

1 teaspoon white rum

1 teaspoon corn syrup

For Mango Layer:

1 cup chopped fresh mango (peeled)

1 tablespoon frozen limeade concentrate

1 teaspoon white rum

1 teaspoon corn syrup

Key limes for garnish

Steps For each layer, puree ingredients in a food processor, and transfer to plastic airtight containers. Freeze until firm.

Spoon 2 tablespoons of each layer into the push pop containers; compacting each layer down for a level surface. Keep frozen until ready to serve. Garnish with a key lime wheel.

Makes 6 - 8 (4 oz.) push pops

Mai Tai Snow Cones

Wishing I was in Hawaii, but happy to dream about the Pacific Island in my backyard enjoying these Mai Tai Snow Cones.

Ingredients

1/4 cup dark rum

1/2 cup pineapple juice

2 tablespoon grenadine

1 1/2 cups sugar

1/2 cup water

Crushed pineapple

Red Maraschino cherries

Snow cone ice

Steps Mix together rum, pineapple juice, and grenadine; set aside.

Combine sugar and water in a small saucepan, and stir until sugar is just moistened. Bring to a boil over medium heat and cook until mixture turns into syrup or registers 235°F on candy thermometer; about 5 – 8 minutes. Remove from heat, allow mixture to stop boiling (about 30 seconds) and stir in rum mixture. Cool completely, and transfer into a bottle fitted with a bartending pour spout.

Dispense snow cone ice from a home-use machine into a small bowl, and then into a Martini or Margarita glass, along with crushed pineapple. Pour syrup over ice, garnish with a cherry, and serve.

Makes about 2 cups snow cone syrup

Mojito Shaved Ice

If there was ever a cocktail that was meant to be poured over shaved ice, it's the Mojito.

Ingredients

2 cups water

2 cups granulated sugar

1 cup mint leaves plus mint leaves for garnish

Juice of 2 limes

1/2 cup rum

Shaved Ice

Steps Combine water, sugar, and 1 cup mint leaves into a saucepan and stir until sugar is just moistened. Heat over medium until sugar dissolves, about 5 – 8 minutes. Cool completely and strain to remove mint leaves.

Stir in lime juice and rum. Transfer into a bottle fitted with a bartending pour spout.

When ready to serve, dispense shaved ice from a home-use machine into a bowl, and then into a wine glass or serving vessel. Pour Mojito syrup over ice in glass, garnish with mint leaves and serve immediately.

Makes about 3 cups syrup

Appletini Sorbet

Pucker Up! This cocktail darling is even better as a sorbet. You could serve this as a dinner party interlude or an intriguing menu option for an hors d'oeuvre only party.

Ingredients

1/2 cup lime juice

1/2 cup water

1 cup simple syrup (recipe page 13)

3 tablespoon Pucker Sour Apple Schnapps

1 tablespoon vodka

Scant drop green food coloring (optional)

Green apple slivers (immersed in lime juice to prevent browning)

Steps Mix together lime juice, water, simple syrup, liquor, and food coloring. Pour into an 8-inch square metal pan and freeze until solid.

Scrape mixture with a spoon to distribute the ice crystals, and refreeze until solid. Scoop and serve in a Martini glass. Garnish with apple slivers.

Makes about 1 pint

Lemon Drop Basil Sorbet

This Lemon Drop Basil Sorbet is sweet and sour; a perfect palate cleanser for an al fresco meal.

Ingredients

2 cups fresh lemon juice

1 1/4 cup simple syrup (recipe page 13)

2 tablespoons vodka

2 tablespoons minced fresh basil leaves, plus whole basil leaves for garnish

Steps Combine lemon juice and simple syrup. Pour into an ice cream maker and process per manufacturer's instructions. After 10 minutes, or when sorbet has thickened, stir in minced basil and vodka and transfer into a plastic container with a lid. Freeze for at least 4 hours or overnight.

When ready to serve, scoop into a Martini glass and garnish with basil leaves.

Makes about 1 1/2 pints

Grasshopper Ice Cream Brownie Sandwiches

Brownies are great ice cream sandwich holders! I recommend baking the brownies, as directed in the recipe, but you could certainly pick up prepared brownies and cut them into an appropriate size as a time-saver.

Ingredients

1 cup whole milk

1 cup heavy cream

4 large egg yolks

1/2 cup granulated sugar

2 tablespoons crème de menthe

1 tablespoon vodka

1/2 cup milk chocolate chips

Brownie mix

1/2 cup each white, green, dark chocolate Candy Melt chips (optional)

Chocolate frosting

Steps Heat milk and cream in a heavy, medium saucepan over medium heat, stirring occasionally, until hot, but do not boil; about 5 minutes. Remove from heat and set aside.

Beat yolks and sugar on low speed in a bowl until combined. Gradually add hot milk-cream into yolk mixture in slow streams to temper eggs. Pour mixture into saucepan and reduce heat to low. Stir constantly until mixture thickens slightly, about 5 minutes, but do not let mixture boil. Strain into medium bowl and refrigerate until chilled, at least 8 hours.

Pour chilled mixture into an ice cream maker and process according to manufacturer's instructions. When the ice cream is almost done processing, add crème de menthe, vodka, and chocolate chips and continue mixing until done. Transfer into a plastic container and freeze overnight.

Bake brownies according to package directions in a 9 X 13 pan lined with wax paper. Cut baked whole brownie sheet in half, making 2 (9 X 6.5) rectangles. Spread Grasshopper ice cream in an even layer on one brownie half, and top with other brownie half. Freeze until ice cream firms up. Then, cut into 2-inch squares and freeze until ready to serve.

To make the marble chocolate garnish on top of the Grasshopper Ice Cream Brownie Sandwiches in the photo, melt white, green, and dark chocolate Candy Melt chips in small bowls. Line a cookie sheet with wax paper and pour melted chips on wax paper. Swirl to create a marbleized look and set aside until firm. Break off pieces of marble chocolate and place on brownies with a dab of chocolate frosting.

Makes about 12 ice cream brownie sandwiches

Irish Cream Ice Cream

This delicious Baileys ice cream is for the White Russian Ice Cream Sliders recipe that follows.

Ingredients

1 cup whole milk

1 cup heavy cream

4 large egg yolks

1/2 cup granulated sugar

2 tablespoons Baileys Original Irish Cream

Steps Heat milk and cream in a heavy, medium saucepan over medium heat, stirring occasionally, until hot, but do not boil; about 5 minutes. Remove from heat and set aside.

Beat yolks and sugar on low speed in a bowl until combined. Gradually add hot milk-cream into yolk mixture in slow streams to temper eggs. Pour back mixture into saucepan and reduce heat to low. Stir constantly until mixture thickens slightly, about 5 minutes, but do not let mixture boil. Strain into medium bowl and refrigerate until chilled, at least 8 hours.

Pour chilled mixture into an ice cream maker and process according to manufacturer's instructions. When the ice cream is almost done processing, add Baileys and continue mixing until done. Transfer into an airtight plastic container and freeze overnight to firm up ice cream.

Makes about 1 pint

White Russian Ice Cream Sandwich Sliders

Petite ice cream sliders with homemade Irish Cream Ice Cream…heavenly!

Ingredients

Black Russian Espresso Cookies

1 cup butter, at room temperature

3/4 cup granulated sugar

3/4 cup golden brown sugar

3 tablespoons espresso powder

3 tablespoons Kahlua

1 tablespoon vodka

2 large eggs

2 cups all-purpose flour

1 teaspoon baking powder

1/4 cup unsweetened cocoa powder

Slivered almonds

Irish Cream Ice Cream (recipe page 36)

Steps Beat butter and sugars in a large bowl until fluffy. Dilute espresso powder in Kahlua, and beat into mixture with vodka and eggs. Sift together flour, baking powder, and cocoa powder, and beat into mixture until combined. Chill dough for 1 hour. Roll dough into 1 1/2-inch diameter logs. Wrap in plastic and chill until firm.

Preheat oven to 350 degrees. Cover a cookie sheet with wax paper and coat lightly with non-stick cooking spray. Slice off 1/4-inch thick rounds from cookie dough log and reform into neat circles. Place on prepared cookie sheet about 2 inches apart. Insert a slivered almond in center of each cookie. Bake for 8 minutes. Remove from oven and cool completely on cookie sheet.

Scoop 2-3 tablespoons of Irish Cream Ice Cream on one cookie and top with another cookie. Smooth around side of ice cream sandwich using a butter knife, and place in the freezer while preparing remaining sandwiches. Cover with plastic wrap and chill until firm before serving.

Makes about 48 cookies; 1 pint of ice cream makes 10 – 12 ice cream sandwich sliders

DINNER PARTY
INDULGENCES

Pistachio and Coffee Liqueur Kulfi Pops

Kulfi is India's version of an ice milk pop. Many kulfi recipes call for sweetened condensed milk, which creates a lovely texture.

Ingredients

1/4 cup strong cold coffee

1/4 cup sweetened condensed milk

1 cup heavy cream

2 tablespoons Kahlua

1/2 teaspoon ground cardamom

1/4 cup finely chopped pistachios (divided)

6 (6-inch long) cinnamon sticks

Steps Mix together coffee, sweetened condensed milk, cream, Kahlua, vodka, cardamom, and 2 tablespoons pistachios.

Fill 6 (2 oz.) plastic molds with mixture, and freeze until slightly firm.

Insert cinnamon sticks and freeze completely.

Remove pops from molds, brush tops with simple syrup (recipe page 13), and sprinkle remaining 2 tablespoons pistachios over syrup on pops.

Serve on ice in a large bowl.

Makes 6 (2 oz.) pops

Peanut Butter Fudge Chunk Banana Push Pops

Who doesn't love chunks of fudge in their ice cream, and the combination of peanut butter, banana, and chocolate is always a winner!

Ingredients

1 tablespoon butter

1 tablespoon sugar

1 banana, sliced into rounds

1/2 cup heavy cream

1/2 cup milk

1/4 cup sweetened condensed milk

2 tablespoons crème de banana

Peanut butter and chocolate fudge chunks (recipe page 43)

Steps Melt butter over medium heat in a small skillet. Add bananas and sauté for 1 minute, then add sugar. Gently stir to coat until sugar is dissolved and bananas deepen in color, about 1 - 2 minutes. Pour bananas and sauce from pan into a medium mixing bowl.

Add cream, milk, sweetened condensed milk, and crème de banana into mixing bowl with bananas. Stir mixture with a fork while mashing bananas until mixture is smooth and incorporated. Transfer mixture to an airtight plastic container, and freeze until firm.

Add 3 peanut butter, 3 chocolate fudge chunks, and 4 tablespoons of banana mixture alternately into push pop containers creating a design similar to the photo. Keep frozen until ready to serve.

Makes 6 (4 oz.) push pops

Peanut Butter and Chocolate Fudge Candy

Good news is, you'll have some fudge left over after using this candy for the Peanut Butter Fudge Chunky Banana Push Pops!

Ingredients

1/3 cup creamy peanut butter

1/3 cup milk chocolate chips

1 cup sugar

1/3 cup evaporated milk

1/4 cup butter

Pinch of salt

1 - 2 tablespoons corn syrup

Steps Put peanut butter in a large bowl and chocolate chips in another large bowl. Line an 8-inch square baking dish with wax paper on the bottom and up the sides.

Stir together sugar, evaporated milk, butter, and salt in a medium heavy bottom saucepan. Bring to a boil over medium heat and cook for about 6-8 minutes, stirring occasionally, until mixture is foamy and thickens. Remove from heat and immediately pour into a 2-cup heat-proof measuring cup.

Pour half of mixture over peanut butter in one mixing bowl and remaining half over chocolate chips in the other bowl. Beat peanut butter mixture on a low speed for 5 minutes and then increase speed to high for another 5 minutes. If mixture seems gritty, add 1 tablespoon of corn syrup until the mixture forms a smooth mass. Repeat steps with remaining mixture and chocolate chips. Pat fudge into wax paper lined dish with peanut fudge on one side of dish and chocolate on the other side. (I also like to use a paper towel and absorb any grease from the fudge. Simply pat the top of the fudge with the towel and then if necessary, smooth the top with your fingers.)

Cover dish and chill until set. Cut 1/2-inch cubes from fudge for the Peanut Butter Fudge Chunk Banana Push Pops.

Makes an 8-inch slab of fudge

Mandarin Orange Gin Pops

My mom is a big fan of Mandarin oranges on salads and the Ramos Fizz cocktail, which features gin. I know it's an oldie but goodie, like my mom, so, this pop is dedicated to her: Jane Benedict!

Ingredients

1 (15 oz.) can Mandarin oranges, packed in syrup

1/2 cup Mandarin orange liquid drained from can

1/2 cup water

1/4 cup simple syrup (recipe page 13)

3 tablespoons fresh lime juice

4 teaspoons gin

Small mint leaves

Steps Mix together Mandarin orange liquid, water, simple syrup, lime juice, and gin.

Fill 6 (2 oz.) plastic molds with mixture and freeze until slushy.

Insert pop sticks when mixture is a firm slush and freeze completely.

Remove pops from molds and adhere a Mandarin orange segment and a small sprig of mint on top of pops using sugar glue (recipe page 13).

Serve upright on ice in a large bowl so garnish stays intact on top of pops.

Makes about 6 (2 oz.) pops

Cherry Bourbon Milkshake Shots

These spiked cherry milkshake shooters get their kick from an ample splash of bourbon!

Ingredients

1 cup cherries, pitted, and 8 cherries for garnish

3 tablespoons bourbon

2 cups vanilla ice cream

2 – 4 oz. dark chocolate

2 – 4 oz. white chocolate

1/4 cup ground graham crackers

Steps Combine 1 cup cherries and bourbon in a food processor, and blend until smooth. Add ice cream and process until combined. Pour into a plastic container and keep covered in freezer.

Cut a slit into garnish cherries so they can rest easily on the rim of a shot glass. Melt dark chocolate in a small bowl in the microwave on the defrost setting. (I usually set the timer to 10 second increments, until the chocolate starts to melt. Then, I stir it and allow it to melt completely in the warm bowl. Chocolate seizes up if it is heated too much.)

Dip each cherry in the melted chocolate, and then slip a knife through the slit to keep it open. Place cherries on wax paper to allow chocolate to set. Melt white chocolate, same as the dark chocolate. Dip the rim of each shot glass in the chocolate, and then graham cracker crumbs.

When ready to serve, stir milkshake mixture to thaw if necessary. Pour milkshakes into prepared shot glasses, and garnish with chocolate-dipped cherry.

Makes about 8 (2 oz.) shots

Kiwi Pomegranate Vodka Pops

While kiwi is seldom used as an ingredient in cocktails, its vibrant green striations dotted with black seeds seems a brilliant choice when paired with pomegranate seeds in a pop.

Ingredients

1 pomegranate

1 cup bottled pomegranate juice

1/4 cup water

1/4 cup simple syrup (recipe page 13)

2 tablespoons vodka

2 kiwi, peeled and cut into 1/8-inch thick slices

Steps Peel open pomegranate and remove seeds. Add 10 seeds each into 6 (2 oz.) plastic pop molds.

Mix together pomegranate juice, water, simple syrup, and vodka.

Fill pop molds 3/4 full with mixture and freeze until slushy; reserve remaining mixture.

Insert pop sticks when mixture is a firm slush and freeze completely.

To get a "window pane" look with kiwi slices, unmold pops and place in freezer to keep firm. Re-fill each mold with 1 tablespoon of reserved mixture. Coat kiwi slices in sugar glue (recipe page 13) and adhere to pops. Submerge pops back in molds so mixture in bottom comes up around kiwi and is level with top surface; freeze completely.

Remove pops from molds and serve on ice in a large bowl.

Makes 6 (2 oz.) pops

Mulled Cider Pops

These pops make me think of fall, tailgating, and Halloween!

Ingredients

1 tablespoon butter

1 tablespoon brown sugar

1 Red Delicious apple (peeled, cored, sliced into thin wedges)

3/4 cup apple cider

1/2 cup water

1/4 cup simple syrup (recipe page 13)

2 tablespoons brandy

1/8 teaspoon ground cinnamon

1/8 teaspoon ground ginger

1/8 teaspoon ground nutmeg

1/8 teaspoon ground cloves

6 (6-inch long) cinnamon sticks

Steps Melt butter and sugar in a small skillet over medium heat. Add apples and sauté until apples are golden brown. Remove from heat and cool completely.

Mix together apple cider, water, simple syrup, brandy, and spices. Fill 6 (2 oz.) pop molds 3/4 full with mixture and freeze until slushy; reserve remaining mixture. Insert cinnamon sticks when mixture is a firm slush and freeze completely.

To get a "window pane" look with apple slices, unmold pops and place in freezer to keep firm. Re-fill each mold with 1 tablespoon of reserved mixture. Coat apple slices in sugar glue (recipe page 13) and adhere to pops. Submerge pops back in molds so mixture in bottom comes up around apples and is level with top surface; freeze completely.

Remove pops from molds and serve on ice in a large bowl.

Makes 6 (2 oz.) pops

Black Russian Pops

Although these spiked coffee pops are in my chapter on dinner party treats, I think they would be a welcome addition on a brunch menu as well.

Ingredients

1 1/4 cups strong cold coffee

1/4 cup simple syrup (recipe page 13)

4 teaspoons Kahlua

2 teaspoons vodka

Sweetened whipped cream

Chocolate-covered espresso beans

Steps Mix together coffee, simple syrup, Kahlua, and vodka.

Fill 6 (2 oz.) plastic molds with mixture and freeze until slushy.

Insert pop sticks when mixture is a firm slush and freeze completely.

Remove pops from molds, place a dab of whipped cream on top, and garnish with a chocolate-covered espresso bean.

Serve upright on ice in a large bowl so garnish stays intact on top of pops.

Makes 6 (2 oz.) pops

Bananas Foster Fudge Pops

The rummy, caramel sauce in the Bananas Foster portion of this recipe mixes with the fudge in the most scrumptious way.

Ingredients

1 tablespoon butter

1/4 cup golden brown sugar

2 tablespoons dark rum

1 banana, sliced into 1/4-inch thick rounds

1 cup milk

1/2 cup hot fudge topping (Smuckers)

Steps Melt butter over medium heat in a small skillet. Add bananas and sauté for 1 minute, then add sugar. Gently stir to coat until sugar is dissolved and bananas deepen in color, about 1 - 2 minutes. Add rum and cook for 30 seconds more. Remove from heat and spoon 2 tablespoons caramel sauce from pan into a small mixing bowl. Transfer bananas to a sheet of wax paper to cool, then cover and set aside.

Warm milk in the microwave for about 10 seconds and add to caramel in bowl. Stir in fudge topping until incorporated. Transfer mixture to a large measuring cup with a pour spout and refrigerate until cold.

Use a pop stick to press a couple of the caramelized bananas inside each mold of a frozen quick pop maker, such as Zoku (for slow pops see "window pane" design tips on page 11). Insert pop sticks. Fill mold with fudge mixture and freeze.

Remove pops from molds, put in plastic bags, and keep in freezer while making more pops. Serve pops on ice in a large bowl.

Makes 6 (2 oz.) pops

Bourbon Caramel Pecan Sundae Push Pops

The star ingredient and only homemade element in this dessert is the bourbon caramel, which is also fantastic as a pie topping.

Ingredients

3/4 cups sugar

3 tablespoons water

1/2 cup heavy cream

2 tablespoons bourbon

8 (2-inch square) brownies

1/2 cup chopped pecans, 8 whole pecans

1 cup vanilla ice cream

Steps Stir together sugar and water in a medium heavy bottom saucepan until just combined. Cook over medium heat for about 6 – 8 minutes until sugar just appears to turn amber. Remove from heat and carefully stir in cream (the addition of cream will cause the caramel to spatter a bit). When cream is incorporated, stir in bourbon. Cool and transfer into a small bowl. Cover and refrigerate until cold.

Use push pop container to stamp out brownies into circles. Place a brownie circle in the bottom of each push pop container.

Drizzle 1 tablespoon of caramel over brownie, add 1 tablespoon chopped pecans, a 2-tablespoon scoop of vanilla ice cream, another drizzle of caramel, and top with a whole pecan. Make remaining push pops and keep frozen until ready to serve.

Makes 1 1/4 cup caramel sauce; 8 (4 oz.) push pops

Soused Strawberry Shortcake Push Pops

This ridiculously easy recipe features Amaretto soused pound cake, but you could easily substitute a similar liqueur that you may have on hand, such as Frangelico, brandy, even a tawny port.

Ingredients

1lb. loaf pound cake, cut into 1-inch thick slices

1/2 cup chopped strawberries, plus 8 sliced strawberries for garnish

2/3 cup Amaretto

Whipped cream (canned)

Steps Place pound cake slices on a flat surface. Stamp out cake circles using push pop containers. Slide each cake circle down into a push pop container as the bottom layer.

For each push pop, add 1 tablespoon chopped strawberries on cake circle and drizzle 1 tablespoon Amaretto over strawberries. Cover each container with a push pop cap or plastic, and freeze for at least 2 hours.

When ready to serve, pipe whipped cream on top of frozen strawberry layer. Add 1 teaspoon of Amaretto over whipped cream, and place a strawberry slice on the edge of the container as a garnish.

Makes 8 (4 oz.) push pops

Orange Cream Cocktail Gelato

This sophisticated treat tastes a lot like a grown-up Creamsicle pop thanks to a welcome addition of vodka.

Ingredients

5 large egg yolks

3/4 cups granulated sugar

1 1/2 cups skim milk (2%)

Peel of an orange cut into strips

1/4 cup orange juice

1/4 cup vodka

1 tablespoon vanilla

Whole oranges

Steps

Whisk together yolks and sugar in a bowl until combined; set aside.

Add milk and orange peel into a heavy bottom, medium saucepan. Cook over medium heat until milk is scalded, but do not boil. Remove orange peels.

Gradually whisk milk into yolk mixture in slow streams to temper eggs. Whisk in orange juice, vodka, and vanilla. Return mixture to saucepan and reduce heat to low. Stir constantly until mixture thickens slightly, about 5 minutes, but do not let mixture boil. Strain into medium bowl and refrigerate until chilled.

Pour chilled mixture into an ice cream maker and process according to manufacturer's instructions. Transfer into an airtight plastic container and freeze overnight to firm up gelato.

Just before serving, cut an orange in half and remove pulp. Place orange half shell into a Margarita glass and add a scoop of gelato into the shell. Garnish with an orange leaf and an orange peel star (made using a mini star cutter).

Makes about 2 1/2 cups

Chocolate Hazelnut Liqueur Gelato

This recipe is a bit pricey, between the Nutella, chocolate bar, and Frangelico. But, I really wanted to make a decadent gelato with a nice depth of flavor that lingers, and it certainly does.

Ingredients

5 large egg yolks

3/4 cups granulated sugar

2 cups whole milk

1/2 cup Nutella

1/4 cup Frangelico hazelnut liqueur

1 (3.5 oz.) chocolate bar, 70% dark cocoa

Pirouette cookies

Steps Whisk together yolks and sugar in a bowl until combined; set aside.

Add milk into a heavy bottom, medium saucepan. Cook over medium heat until milk is scalded, but do not boil.

Gradually whisk milk into yolk mixture in slow streams to temper eggs. Return mixture to saucepan and reduce heat to low. Stir constantly until mixture thickens slightly, about 5 minutes, but do not let mixture boil. Strain into medium bowl. Stir in Nutella, chocolate, and Frangelico until mixture is smooth. Cover and refrigerate until chilled.

Pour chilled mixture into an ice cream maker and process according to manufacturer's instructions. Transfer into an airtight plastic container and freeze overnight to firm up gelato.

Just before serving, scoop gelato into a Martini glass and garnish with a pirouette cookie.

Makes about 3 cups

Peppermint Schnapps Pops

Pure peppermint freeze is what you'll get from these pops, and their rustic rosemary sticks make them an intriguing choice for a holiday cocktail party.

Ingredients

1 cup water

1/3 cup simple syrup (recipe pg. 13)

3 tablespoons peppermint schnapps

1/4 teaspoon peppermint extract

6 (8-inch long) rosemary stems (use thick stems)

Steps Mix together water, simple syrup, peppermint schnapps, and extract.

Fill 6 (2 oz.) pop molds with mixture and freeze until slushy.

Strip needles from bottom of rosemary stems to where needles are on a 3-inch portion of the tip. Insert rosemary stems, with needles in mold, when mixture is a firm slush; freeze completely.

Remove pops from molds, and serve on ice in a large bowl.

Makes 6 (2 oz.) pops

NYE Raspberry Pop Swizzle Sticks in Champagne

This Champagne cocktail pop is perfect for a brunch. Serve the Raspberry Pop Swizzle Sticks on ice next to a bottle of Champagne and flutes for guests to grab and plunge into some bubbly.

Ingredients

1 cup fresh or frozen raspberries

1 tablespoon water

1 tablespoon Chambord liqueur

1 teaspoon sugar

16 plastic swizzle sticks

Champagne

Steps Puree raspberries, water, liqueur, and sugar in a blender until smooth. Transfer into an airtight plastic container and freeze overnight until firm.

Prepare a metal or foil-lined tray for pops to set up. And, clear a space in your freezer for the tray, allowing for the height of the swizzle sticks.

Form balls from raspberry mixture using a 1-tablespoon measuring spoon. Insert swizzle sticks into raspberry balls, reforming balls if necessary to compact them around sticks. Place on prepared tray and keep tray in freezer while making new pop swizzle sticks. Freeze pops until solid.

When ready to serve, place pops on ice in a bowl next to Champagne and glass flutes. Invite guests to pour Champagne into their flutes and stir with a raspberry pop swizzle stick.

Makes 16 swizzle stick pops

Valentine's Day Chocolate Cherry Bonbons

Playing with chocolate can have such stunning results! For these bonbons, I recommend using Wilton's Candy Melts, colored "faux chocolate" wafers that melt easily in the microwave.

Ingredients

Eggies plastic cups for molds

12 oz. bag Dark Chocolate Candy Melts

12 oz. bag White Chocolate Candy Melts

12 oz. bag Red Chocolate Candy Melts

1 cup vanilla ice cream

2 tablespoons kirshwasser brandy

1/2 chopped red cherries

Steps For the bonbon molds, I used Eggies plastic cups (a product meant for microwaving eggs). Lightly coat inside Eggie cups with vegetable oil.

Melt 1/4 cup red Candy Melts in the microwave for 20-second increments on defrost setting. Use a pop stick to make red heart design in molds. Freeze molds 5 minutes to set hearts.

Melt 1 cup dark chocolate Candy Melts. Add 2 tablespoons melted chocolate into each mold with a heart and swirl mold around so chocolate completely and evenly coats the inside. For white and dark chocolate marble design, add 1 tablespoon melted white chocolate Candy Melts in molds and use a pop stick to swirl chocolates together. Freeze until chocolate sets. Gently unmold chocolate, as it is too difficult with ice cream in bonbons, and put chocolate shells loosely back into molds.

Mix together vanilla ice cream, kirshwasser, and cherries until combined. Fill chocolate shells with ice cream leaving space at the top for final chocolate layer. Melt 1/2 cup dark chocolate and spoon 1 tablespoon each on top of ice cream in shell. Spread chocolate to edges creating a seal with chocolate shell. Freeze completely. When ready to serve, unmold bonbons, and place on cold plates.

Makes 8 bonbons

St. Patrick's Day Irish Breakfast Pops

A "magically delicious" treat, these pops get a double dose of Irish luck with both Baileys and Lucky Charms cereal as ingredients!

Ingredients

1 cup whole milk

1/3 cup simple syrup (recipe page 13)

2 tablespoons Baileys Original Irish Cream

Lucky Charms Cereal

Steps Mix together milk, simple syrup, and Baileys.

Insert pop sticks inside each mold of a frozen quick pop maker, such as Zoku. Pour mixture into molds and freeze.

Remove pops from molds, put in plastic bags, and keep in freezer while decorating each pop. Adhere Lucky Charms cereal to pop using sugar glue (recipe page 13). Place pops back in freezer to help sugar glue set.

 Serve pops on ice in a large bowl.

Makes 6 (2 oz.) pops

Shamrock Cucumber Lime Pops

Cucumber is one of my favorite flavorings for vodka. Even though I've made this a holiday recipe with the shamrock shape, this pop is terrific any time of year, substituting a cucumber circle, for a cocktail party.

Ingredients

1 cup water

1/4 cup fresh lime juice

1/4 cup simple syrup (recipe page 13)

2 tablespoons cucumber-flavored vodka

6-inch piece of cucumber, peeled and cut into 1/8-inch thick slices

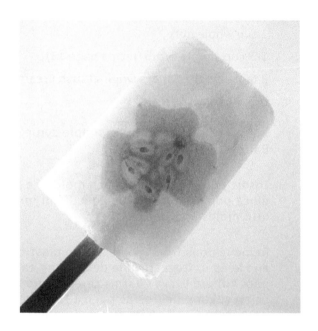

Steps Mix together water, lime juice, simple syrup, and vodka.

Fill 6 (2 oz.) pop molds 3/4 full with mixture and freeze until slushy; reserve remaining mixture.

Insert pop sticks when mixture is a firm slush and freeze completely.

Use an appropriate-sized shamrock cookie cutter to cut out shamrock shapes from cucumber slices. To get a "window pane" look with cucumber slices, unmold pops and place in freezer to keep firm. Re-fill each mold with 1 tablespoon of reserved mixture. Coat cucumber shamrock slices in sugar glue (recipe page 13) and adhere to pops. Submerge pops back in molds so mixture in bottom comes up around shamrock cucumbers and is level with top surface; freeze completely.

Remove pops from molds and serve on ice in a large bowl.

Makes 6 (2 oz.) pops

Easter Egg Pops

What a fun pop for the Easter holiday, especially on a brunch bar! Make sure that the kids know these pops have vodka in them, and you can omit the vodka for an alcohol-free version of this treat.

Ingredients

6 flexible plastic Easter Eggs that come apart in the middle and have a water-tight seal when halves are together (test them!)

Empty egg carton

1 1/4 cup water

1/3 cup simple syrup (recipe page 13)

2 flavors powdered Kool-Aid drink mix packets

2 teaspoons vodka (divided)

Steps Make sure the egg molds are a flexible plastic or they could crack. Assemble eggs. Make a 1/4-inch diameter hole in the center of the wider end of the egg. I used a Dremel, high speed drill, but you could also use a nail or a sharp knife (be careful).

Open the eggs and pull away excess plastic from where you made the hole. Wash the eggs with hot, soapy water; rinse and dry completely. Tape any small holes at the narrow end on the outside of the egg with small pieces of strong tape. Assemble eggs.

Mix together water and simple syrup. Divide mixture into 2 bowls. Add 1/8 – 1/4 teaspoon of drink mix and 1 teaspoon vodka into each bowl. Stir until drink mix dissolves. Transfer each mixture into a spouted container to fill egg molds or you could use a small funnel. Fill each egg mold over the sink; wipe off drips on the outside. Place in eggs in an egg carton (fill hole side on top), and freeze until solid.

To unmold egg pops, twist off narrow ends of plastic egg halves, and use wide plastic egg halves as the pop holders. Serve embedded in crushed ice in a bowl.

Makes 6 (2 oz.) pops

Kentucky Derby Mint Julep Pops

The Kentucky Derby is my favorite sporting event. Short, sweet, and a signature drink! I used a Zoku Quick Pop Maker and Zoku Tools Kit to make these pops. In this recipe, I reference items in their Tools kit, which consists of: spouted pour cups with oz. measurements on the side, fruit wand to apply items inside the mold, siphon, and mini shape cutters.

Ingredients

1 1/4 cup cold water

1/4 cup simple syrup (recipe page 13)

1/2 cup mint leaves (divided)

1 tablespoon bourbon

1 tablespoon cola

Steps Mix together water and simple syrup. Coarsely chop 1/4 cup mint leaves and add to mixture. Cover and refrigerate for 2 or more hours to infuse mint into syrup.

Strain syrup to remove mint leaves. Divide syrup into 2 Zoku pour cups or spouted containers. Mix cola into one cup and bourbon into the other cup.

Tilt a frozen Zoku Quick Pop Maker on the angle tray from the Zoku Tools Kit. Insert pop sticks. Fill each mold with 1 oz. of cola mixture and freeze. Place pop on a flat surface and use the Zoku fruit wand or pop stick to insert a few of the remaining mint leaves down into the each mold. Fill remainder of molds with bourbon mixture and freeze.

Remove pops from molds, put in plastic bags, and keep in freezer while making more pops. Serve pops on ice in a large bowl.

Makes 6 (2 oz.) pops

Cinco De Mayo Frozen Mexi-Coco Mousse Cookie Tacos

Fortune cookie origami! I was tickled when I came up with the idea of heating a fortune cookie and reshaping it into a taco. It is so simple and makes a dynamite presentation!

Ingredients

Frozen Mexi-Coco Mousse

4 oz. dark chocolate, chopped

2 large egg yolks

2 tablespoons granulated sugar

2 tablespoons Kahlua

1 cup heavy whipping cream, cold

3 large egg whites

1 teaspoon ground cinnamon

Fortune Cookie Tacos

12 fortune cookies

2 – 4 oz. dark chocolate

1/4 cup chopped pistachio nuts

12 dried banana chips

12 raspberries

Steps To make mousse, melt dark chocolate in a double boiler. Cool 5 minutes. Beat egg yolks and sugar in a large bowl until thickened. Beat in melted chocolate and Kahlua. Using clean beaters, whip cream in a metal bowl until thick; fold into egg mixture. Using clean beaters, beat egg whites in another bowl until stiff peaks form. Fold egg whites and cinnamon into mixture until blended. Cover and freeze until firm.

Heat each fortune cookie in the microwave for 20 seconds or until it begins to open. Gently open cookie and press down in the center to form a taco shell. Repeat process with all cookies. When cookies harden again, melt dark chocolate, and dip cookie edges in chocolate, then pistachio nuts.

When ready to serve, spoon mousse in cookie tacos and garnish with banana chips and raspberries.

Makes 12 cookie tacos

Mother's Day Mimosa Blackberry Peach Push Pops

This pop is a perfect Mother's Day afternoon repast, between breakfast in bed and going out to dinner with the family. Laguna Wholesale is where you'll find the heart push pops containers.

Ingredients

Peach Mimosa Push Pops

1 (15 oz.) can peaches in heavy syrup (drained)

1/2 cup Champagne

3 tablespoons corn syrup

Blackberry Brandy Syrup Swirl

1/2 cup sugar

1/4 cup fresh or frozen blackberries

2 tablespoons blackberry brandy

2 teaspoons corn syrup

Steps To make Peach Mimosa mixture, puree ingredients in a food processor, and transfer to a plastic airtight container; freeze.

To make Blackberry Brandy Syrup Swirl, add sugar, blackberries, and brandy into a small saucepan. Mash blackberries with a fork to release their juices; stir mixture to combine. Cook over medium heat for 5 minutes until sugar dissolves. Strain mixture into a small bowl to remove blackberry seeds. Stir in corn syrup, cover, and allow to thicken overnight. (I added the corn syrup after the cooking process, because I found that it gave the blackberry swirl a richer color, and the texture was easier to spread in the mold.)

Use a pop stick to spread blackberry syrup swirl in a whimsical design inside the push pop containers. Freeze for 10 minutes. Then, spoon frozen peach mixture into molds. Finish off the push pops with a swirl of blackberry syrup on top. Put pops back in the freezer until firm.

Serve pops on ice in a bowl or ice bucket.

Makes 6 (4 oz.) push pops

Father's Day Whiskey Sour Pops

There's something about the classic Whiskey Sour cocktail that feels like a "dad" drink and a cherry on top seems more than apropos to a guy who is everything to so many. Of course, this pop is dedicated to my dear dad.

Ingredients

1 cup liquid sweet and sour mixer

1/2 cup water

2 tablespoons whiskey

1/4 cup cola

6 Maraschino cherries

Steps Mix together sweet and sour mixer, water, and whiskey. Divide mixture into 2 bowls. Stir cola into one of the bowls.

Fill 6 (2 oz.) plastic molds 1/2 full with cola mixture and freeze. Fill remainder of molds with other mixture and freeze to a firm slush.

Insert pop sticks and when mixture is a firm slush, then freeze completely.

Remove pops from molds and adhere Maraschino cherries on top of pops using sugar glue (recipe page 13).

Serve upright on ice in a large bowl so garnish stays intact on top of pops.

Makes about 6 (2 oz.) pops

July 4th Patriotic Margarita Pops

These Patriotic Pops are one of my favorites that I shared on the Today Show. I made them with the Zoku Quick Pop Maker and Tools Kit (see page 69 head notes preceding Kentucky Derby Mint Julep for more info about Zoku products).

Ingredients

1 cup cold water

1/3 cup fresh lemon juice

3 tablespoons sugar

2 tablespoons Tequila

Red & blue food coloring

1 Macintosh apple, cut into 1/8-inch slices, in lemon juice to prevent browning

Steps Combine water, lemon juice, sugar, and Tequila in a bowl. Divide mixture into 3 pour cups from Zoku Tools Kit. Tint one mixture red and tint another mixture blue.

To make the pop design in the photo, stamp out Macintosh apple stars from slices using the mini star cutter in the Tools Kit. Then, use the fruit wand to adhere stars inside the molds of the pop maker.

Insert pop sticks into the molds. Tilt pop maker on the angle tray in the Tools Kit. Use the siphon in the Tools Kit to add 1 tablespoon of red mixture into each pop mold; freeze. Tilt the pop maker the other direction on the angle tray and use the siphon to add 1 tablespoon of white or clear mixture on the opposite side from the red; freeze. Place pop maker on flat surface and pour blue mixture into each mold to fill line; freeze.

Remove pops from molds, put in plastic bags, and keep in freezer while making more pops. Serve pops on ice in a large bowl.

Makes 6 (2 oz.) pops

Halloween Candy Corn Cocktail Push Pops

This cocktail pop concoction is a simple one, but with its famous Halloween candy theme, it is sure to be a big hit at any fright night fest!

Ingredients

1 (9X13) loaf cake dyed yellow with gel food coloring

3 cups vanilla ice cream

3 tablespoons Baileys Irish Cream Liqueur

Orange gel food coloring

1 container white frosting (not whipped or fluffy)

Candy corn

Steps Crumble yellow cake. Mix together 1 cup cake crumbs with 1 cup vanilla ice cream and 1 tablespoon Baileys until thoroughly combined. Fill push pop containers 1/4 full with mixture and place upright in the freezer for 30 minutes or until solid.

Meanwhile, combine 2 cups vanilla ice cream with 2 tablespoons of Baileys. Add orange gel food coloring until desired color is achieved. (Taste test throughout to make sure you don't go overboard and get that awful food coloring taste.)

Remove push pop containers from freezer and add orange ice cream on top of frozen cake layer to 3/4 full in container. (Tip: If the cake isn't frozen, the orange ice cream will seep down the sides inside the container ruining the layered look.) Freeze until solid.

Mix 1 cup frosting with 1 tablespoon Baileys. Dollop frosting on orange ice cream, and top it with candy corn. Place back in freezer for about 15 minutes to allow frosting to chill and then serve.

Makes about 12 (4 oz.) push pops

Halloween Creepy Cosmo Pops with Gummy Bugs

I am super excited about these creepy pops! I've been experimenting with gummy candy and making custom molds using food-grade silicone putty from the company Make Your Own Molds. Visit JeanneBenedict.com for an in-depth tutorial on making these molds and the gummy bugs.

Ingredients

1 cup white cranberry juice

1/4 cup water

1/3 cup simple syrup (recipe page 13)

1 teaspoon vodka

1 teaspoon triple sec or orange liqueur

1 teaspoon fresh lime juice

Homemade Gummy Bugs

3 tablespoons granulated sugar

2 tablespoons cold water

1 (1/4 oz.) envelope Knox unflavored gelatin

1/4 teaspoon unsweetened cocoa powder

Steps Mix together cranberry juice, water, simple syrup, vodka, triple sec, and lime juice. Fill 6 (2 oz.) pop molds with mixture and freeze until slushy. Insert pop sticks when mixture is firm slush and freeze completely.

You can buy gummy bugs or make them! I made molds using bug toys and food-safe Silicone Plastique® from MakeYourOwnMolds.com. For the gummy mixture, slowly stir ingredients in a heat-proof measuring cup. Cover with plastic wrap and let stand for 10 minutes; remove plastic. Place measuring cup in small saucepan filled halfway with water. Heat mixture in measuring cup over medium heat, slowly stirring occasionally, until water boils and mixture is melted; a spoon dipped in and lifted out should form a sticky thread; about 10 minutes. Carefully remove measuring cup from water. Spoon mixture into bug molds and remove gummy bugs when set.

Moisten underside of bugs, place on pops, and return to freezer until bugs stick to pops. Serve pops on ice in a large bowl using crushed Oreo cookies as edible dirt if desired!

Makes 6 (2 oz.) pops

Thanksgiving Pumpkin Bourbon Dulce le Leche Sherbet

Dulce le leche, a soft caramel made by slowly heating milk and sugar, is absolutely magnificent paired with the autumn flavor of pumpkin.

Ingredients

1 (14 oz.) can sweetened condensed milk (divided)

1/2 cup granulated sugar

1 1/2 cups milk

1 (15 oz.) can Libby's pure pumpkin

3 tablespoons golden brown sugar

3 tablespoons bourbon

Steps Add 1/4 cup sweetened condensed milk into a medium saucepan along with granulated sugar, milk, and pumpkin. Heat over medium heat, stirring often, until mixture is hot and ingredients are combined, but do not allow to boil. Remove from heat and stir in brown sugar and bourbon. Cool to room temperature, then cover and refrigerate until cool.

Meanwhile, make dulce le leche. Preheat oven to 425 degrees. Place remainder of sweetened condensed milk into a 6-inch square casserole dish (or something similar) and cover with foil. Place covered dish in a metal baking pan and fill pan with water halfway up outside of casserole dish. Bake for 1 hour 30 minutes. Carefully lift foil (it will be steamy!) and check the milk's color. If the milk has caramelized into a medium brown, carefully remove from the oven. If more baking time is needed, cook for 15 minutes more and then remove from heat. Cool to room temperature.

Pour cooled pumpkin sherbet batter into ice cream maker and process according to manufacturer's instructions. Layer pumpkin sherbet with swirls of dulce le leche into a plastic container with a lid, and freeze for at least 2 hours before serving.

Makes about 2 1/2 pints

Holiday Baked Alaska Cupcakes

Meringue on pies and cupcakes always reminds me of snow-topped mountains, and snow is so very on theme for the winter holidays!

Ingredients

8 chocolate cupcakes (baked in foil cups for best results)

1 pint mint chocolate chip ice cream

2 tablespoons crème de menthe

4 egg whites

1/2 cup granulated sugar

Steps Scoop out a ping-pong ball size of cake from the center of the cupcakes. (Make sure you don't scrape the bottom of the cupcake.) Mix together ice cream and crème de menthe. Fill the holes with ice cream. Line a baking sheet with foil and put the cupcakes on it; freeze for at least an hour.

Preheat oven to 500F and center the rack in your oven. Whip egg whites on high speed in a dry, clean bowl until they start to stiffen. Gradually add sugar, while beating constantly, until the egg whites form very stiff peaks.

Remove cupcakes from freezer and dollop meringue on top of each cupcake making sure to seal around the edges of the ice cream holes, insulating the ice cream. Smooth and swirl the meringue as you apply it, as opposed to making pointy tips, which burn easily in the oven. (Tip: Keep the foil baking cups on during this process as it helps keep the cupcake and ice cream cold. Then, remove the foil prior to baking the meringue.) Place the baking sheet with the cupcakes in the oven for 2 minutes until the meringue browns. Watch them bake as they can easily burn.

Remove the cupcakes from the oven and serve immediately. Guests can eat these fire and ice delectables with their hands in traditional cupcake style, or plated with a spoon as an elegant dinner party dessert.

Makes 8 cupcakes

Christmas Frozen White Chocolate Egg Nog Mousse

Making mousse can be time-consuming, but this elegant dessert is always worth it.

Ingredients

4 oz. good quality white chocolate, chopped

2 large egg yolks

2 tablespoons granulated sugar

2 tablespoons dark rum

1 cup heavy whipping cream, cold

3 large egg whites

1 teaspoon freshly grated nutmeg

1/4 cup crushed candy canes

Steps Melt white chocolate in a double boiler until smooth. Cool 5 minutes. Beat egg yolks and sugar in a large mixing bowl until thick and pale yellow. Add melted chocolate and rum beat until blended. Using clean beaters, whip cream in a small metal bowl until thick and fold into egg mixture. Using clean beaters, beat egg whites in another small bowl until stiff peaks form. Fold egg whites and nutmeg in yolk mixture. Cover and freeze until firm and ready to use.

Spoon mousse into individual serving dishes and top with crushed candy cane. Serve immediately.

Makes about 1 3/4 – 2 cups

CHILLY CREATIVITY

Hawaiian Sunset with Black Gummy Palm Tree Pops

Food isn't my only artistic outlet. I paint too, and make food dresses (but that's another book). While painting a tropical backdrop for a theater production, I was inspired to create these pops.

Ingredients

1/2 cup water

1/2 cup orange juice

1/2 cup pineapple juice

2 tablespoons rum

2 tablespoons simple syrup (page 13)

1 tablespoon grenadine

Blue food coloring

Black Gummy Palm Trees

1/4 cup sugar

1 tablespoon gelatin

2 tablespoons cold water

1/8 teaspoon black gel food coloring

Steps Mix together water, orange and pineapple juice, and rum. Distribute mixture evenly into 3 bowls. Stir 1 tablespoon simple syrup each into two of the bowls. Stir 1 tablespoon grenadine into the remaining bowl.

Fill 6 (2 oz.) plastic molds 1/3 full with the red grenadine mixture and freeze until solid. Fill molds 2/3 full with bowl of plain mixture, which will be yellow, and freeze to a firm slush. Insert pop sticks and freeze until solid. Tint final bowl of mixture blue, fill molds to the top, and freeze.

To make Black Gummy Palm Trees, slowly mix together sugar, gelatin, and water in a heat-proof measuring cup. Cover with plastic wrap, and set aside for 10 minutes. Fill a small saucepan 1/3 full of water and bring to a boil. Remove plastic wrap from measuring cup and place cup in saucepan of boiling water. Heat gelatin mixture, stirring gently and occasionally, for 8 to 10 minutes until a spoon dipped into mixture creates a bouncy thread when pulled out of mixture. Carefully remove measuring cup from water. Stir in black food coloring and immediately pour mixture on to a dinner plate with a smooth surface. The mixture will spread a bit into an @8-inch wide shape. Allow mixture to set, about 2 hours.

Lightly spray the tip of a sharp knife with non-stick cooking spray. Place the gummy shape on a cutting board and cut out 4-inch long palm tree shapes for each pop. They don't have to be perfect!

Unmold pops and use sugar glue (recipe page 13) to adhere palm trees to the pops. Place pops back in freezer, on a piece of foil or in a metal pan, to firm up glue so palm trees will freeze on to pops. Serve pops on ice in a large bowl.

Makes 6 (2 oz.) pops

Vodka, Watermelon, and Mint Snow Cones

This adult version of a carnival favorite is the ultimate refresher on a hot day.

Ingredients

1 cup water

1 cup sugar

1 cup watermelon, crushed

1 teaspoon lemon juice

1/4 cup vodka

Fresh mint sprigs

Steps Add water, sugar, watermelon, and lemon juice into a small saucepan, and cook over medium-high heat until mixture boils; about 5-8 minutes. Cool completely, strain, and transfer to a bowl. Stir in vodka. Cover and refrigerate until ready to use.

Use a funnel to transfer watermelon syrup into a bottle fitted with a bartending pour spout. Dispense snow cone ice from a home-use machine into a bowl, and then transfer into a Martini glass. Pour 2 tablespoons watermelon syrup on top of each snow cone. Garnish with a mint sprig.

Makes about 2 cups syrup

Frozen Gummy Shot Glasses

Yes, you can buy gummy shot glasses, but making them is so much fun and really easy. The best part about serving a shot in something edible and tasty is that the flavor is a built-in mixer.

Ingredients

1 (6 oz.) box lime gelatin dessert

1/2 cup water

3 (1/4 oz.) envelopes unflavored gelatin

Air Heads Extremes Rainbow Sour Candy Strips

Fred "Cool Shooters" silicone shot glass mold, makes 4 (2.66 oz.) glasses

Premium vodka or Tequila

Steps Mix together lime gelatin, water, and unflavored gelatin in a heat-proof measuring cup. Cover with plastic wrap, and set aside for 10 minutes.

Fill a small saucepan about 1/3 full of water and bring to a boil. Remove plastic wrap from measuring cup and place cup in saucepan of boiling water. Heat gelatin mixture, stirring gently and occasionally, for 8 to 10 minutes until a spoon dipped into mixture creates a bouncy thread when pulled out of mixture.

Carefully remove measuring cup from water. After 1 minute, pour into shot glass mold, evenly disturbing mixture into 4 mold cavities. Cool completely. Then, pull shot glasses out of mold and freeze.

When ready to serve, slide Rainbow Sour Candy Strips on to green plastic picks and insert into the side of the shot glasses. Fill glasses with Tequila or vodka for guests to enjoy!

Makes 4 gummy shot glasses

Bubblegum Word Pops

Bubblegum flavor is instantly fun, and these pop art treats are beyond cool.

Ingredients

1 pack Extra Long-Lasting Flavor Classic Bubble Gum (15 stick count)

1/3 cup simple syrup (recipe page 13)

1 cup water

4 teaspoons vodka

Steps Place 8 sticks of Extra Long-Lasting Flavor Bubble Gum in a bowl of simple syrup. Loosely cover with plastic wrap and steep overnight to infuse pink color and flavor into syrup. Discard gum.

Mix together bubble gum syrup, water, and vodka.

Fill 6 (2 oz.) pop molds 3/4 full with mixture and freeze until slushy; reserve remaining mixture.

Insert pop sticks when mixture is a firm slush and freeze completely.

Use food-safe culinary snips or scissors to cut out letters and shapes from remaining bubble gum sticks (refer to photo.)

Unmold pops and place in freezer to keep firm. Re-fill each mold with 1 tablespoon of reserved mixture. Coat bubble gum letters in sugar glue (recipe page 13) and adhere to pops. Submerge pops back in molds so mixture in bottom comes up around letters and is level with top surface. Use a skewer to straighten or adjust letters in mold if necessary. Freeze completely.

Remove pops from molds and serve on ice in a large bowl.

Makes 6 (2 oz.) pops

Pineapple Flower Ginger Rum Sorbet

Pineapple flowers are so gorgeous, that I was compelled to create a spiked frozen treat to feature them.

Ingredients

1 whole pineapple to make flowers

2 cups fresh chopped pineapple

1 1/4 cup simple syrup (recipe page 13)

1 tablespoon lemon juice

1/4 cup white rum

1 tablespoon minced ginger

Steps Use a knife to remove outer brown skin from pineapple, and cut off about 2 inches from top end; where green spiny leaves are. Also, cut out brown "eyes" left from skin. Slice off pineapple rounds as thin as possible. Place on tray(s) in a food dehydrator and dry at time and temperature suggested by manufacturer for fruit.

To make sorbet, add 2 cups of chopped pineapple into a food processor and puree. Stir in simple syrup, lemon juice, rum, and ginger. Pour mixture into an ice cream maker and process per manufacturer's instructions. After 10 minutes or when sorbet has thickened, transfer into a plastic container with a lid. Freeze for at least 4 hours or overnight.

When ready to serve, scoop sorbet into a Martini glass and garnish with a pineapple flower. Store extra pineapple flowers in a plastic bag at room temperature for up to 1 week.

Makes about 1 pint

A Rainbow of Ice Shot Glasses

Perhaps the best part of this recipe is that the rainbow pop shot glasses are made with sugar-free lemonade, so these are "diet" and delicious! What I found, after much experimentation on these shot glasses, was that the mold is really important. A flexible silicone mold, such as the Fred "Cool Shooter" mold, is great as you can easily slide the mold off the frozen shot glasses. I made these glasses for an Olympics Party to watch the opening ceremony.

Ingredients:

Fred "Cool Shooters" silicone shot glass mold; makes 4 (2.66 oz.) glasses

1 1/3 cup diet lemonade

Assorted Food Colors

Vodka or Tequila

Key lime slices for garnish

Steps Add food coloring to 1/3 cup diet lemonade until desired color is achieved and stir. Pour into shot glass mold cavity. Repeat process with different colors and freeze until solid.

Unmold shot glasses, and garnish each with a key lime slice. Serve shot glasses on ice alongside a bottle of vodka or Tequila so guests can pour themselves a shot. You can make these ahead of time, unmold, and keep them in your freezer until ready to use.

Makes 4 ice shot glasses

Margarita Freezer Pops

You can make the freezer bags for these pops using a food sealer, or buy a box of freezer pops at the 99-cent store, empty out the bags, wash in warm water, and up-cycle the bags for your homemade booze pops!

Ingredients

1 cup liquid Margarita mixer

1/2 cup water

2 tablespoons Tequila

1 tablespoon triple sec

Green food coloring

6 (2 oz.) plastic freezer bags

Corn husk strings

Steps Mix together Margarita mixer, water, Tequila, and triple sec.

Place all freezer bags in a plastic container to keep them upright in the freezer. Use a funnel to fill bags 1/2 full with mixture and freeze until slushy.

Tint remaining Margarita mixture green with food coloring. When mixture in bags is slushy, add green mixture and freeze until firm to give pops a two-tone look.

Corn husks are available in most grocery stores that have a Latin section, as they are used for tamales. Soak corn husks in hot water for 10 seconds to soften and then pull husks apart to make strings. Tie strings around the top of the freezer pop bag and knot; trim excess string.

When ready to serve, insert pops into a bowl or crushed ice.

Makes 6 (2 oz.) freezer pops

Sonic Gin and Tonic Glow in the Dark Pops

Vitamin B2 or Riboflavin, found at most Whole Foods stores in capsule form, glows in the dark or under a black light. Some suggest that quinine, or tonic water has the same luminescence as B2, but I have not found that to be true. However, B2 is very bitter so it works well with tonic-based drinks. Try this for Halloween or a modern cocktail party. It's really awesome!

Ingredients

1 1/2 cup cups tonic water

1/2 cup water

1/3 cup simple syrup (recipe page 13)

6 teaspoons gin

2 tablespoons fresh lime juice

1 (50 mg) B2 or Riboflavin capsule

12 lime peel slivers

Steps Mix together tonic water, water, simple syrup, gin, and lime juice. Open B2 capsule and empty powdered contents into mixture; stir to incorporate.

Pour mixture into cavities of a Tovolo King Ice Cubes silicone mold and freeze until slushy.

I used tongue depressors cut in half for the pop sticks. Be sure to sand cut end of sticks and then wash them to ensure clean, smooth tips.

When mixture is a firm slush, add lime slivers down into the molds, pressing them against the sides so they are visible when pops are unmolded. Then, insert pop sticks and freeze completely.

Unmold pops and serve on ice in a large bowl.

Makes 6 (4 oz.) pops

Note: This is the only ice pop in the book that doesn't have a photo, because black light photos in print look cheesy. But, the photo will be on JeanneBenedict.com, and in digital book and ebook versions.

Passion Fruit Mojito Pops

I spied a bottle of passion fruit juice while shopping. The pale pink color seemed so perfect for an ice pop, and then I thought....Mojito. Enjoy!

Ingredients

3/4 cup passion fruit juice

1/2 cup water

1/4 cup simple syrup (recipe page 13)

1 tablespoon fresh lime juice

1 tablespoon white rum

1/2 cup mint leaves

Steps Mix together passion fruit juice, water, simple syrup, lime juice, and rum.

Fill 6 (2 oz.) plastic molds 3/4 full with mixture and freeze until slushy; reserve remaining mixture.

Insert pop sticks when mixture is a firm slush and freeze completely.

To get a "window pane" look with mint leaves, unmold pops and place in freezer to keep firm. Re-fill each mold with 1 tablespoon of reserved mixture. Coat mint leaves in sugar glue (recipe page 13) and adhere to pops. Submerge pops back in molds so mixture in bottom comes up around mint leaves and is level with top surface; freeze completely.

Remove pops from molds and serve on ice in a large bowl.

Makes 6 (2 oz.) pops

Index

CPSIA information can be obtained at www.ICGtesting.com
Printed in the USA
LVOW02s2203171213

365814LV00004B/22/P